THAT BOOK

My journey to Healing

**By
Gregory Bryers**

FORE WORD

There are people that come and touch us, some to our very souls and then move on while others will quietly walk beside us for many many years. There are many that I thank every day for being there when this angry young boy and man was trying to make his way. They gave me sanctuary from the storms with those quiet words of encouragement, love and wisdom that kept me safe. Some have passed over and I still hear them whisper to me as I struggle with those demons within and the perceived demons without. Thank you! Thank you! Thank you! With all my heart and being, I am grateful for you coming into my life at the times that you have. So... to this I will start.

MAKING MY WAY AS A BOY...

Before I start, I need to say that this is about me, and my perceptions, not only as an adult but as a boy trying to make his way in this screwed up world. I know my sisters have different memories but perhaps this is because they were looking in from their perceptions, coloured by their understandings and knowing's of people looking through younger eyes and minds. This is not to say what they saw, perceived, understood or remember isn't true but that they looked at, and saw from a differing part of the painting.

Something else, should be looked at, and addressed here at the beginning. Something I have always in some way known is that this isn't all there is to life. After my grandmother (aka Dudie), took over the raising of us four kids, she joined the Latter Saints Church, or Mormons. This was, when I look back, what probably saved my life and kept me sane.

My sisters and I excelled in the church youth programs and took to the teachings, scriptures and so

Gregory D Bryers MSc.

forth with understanding and knowing. As teens Jenny and I competed in scripture mastery in seminary (a youth bible class for want of a better description) and we were more often than not at the forefront in leadership roles within the various youth programs.

The church taught that we choose our parents, we choose the situations we are going to be born into. This instils an understanding and acceptance of pre-birth awareness and existence. We don't just spring into existence and know and then wink out at death. We are also taught we are here to learn and experience things we can't as spiritual (energetic infinite) beings.

I liked reading, and discovered that a number of indigenous cultures believed in a cycle of life. We come here and are given things to learn and overcome, then we pass over to study what we learn before coming back to experience new or different experiences…and on the cycle goes. This to me has made the most sense of all the "stuff" I have studied. It is also a teaching that sits very light in my being. So, with this I will address a major question and learning before I talk about the journey … this time.

"Understanding" and "knowing" that I chose my parents and family, to which I was born into, puts the responsibility of what happens in my life squarely back on my shoulders. Knowing that I chose to have a father who was angry and controlling (and everything else negative and positive – he did have many good traits too). That I chose to have a mum that would soon be absent in my life was also my choice. This means, I can't blame anyone anymore.

When this knowing finally cemented itself into my being, I was able to thank my father and move on. That doesn't mean I don't get angry, and carry crap that still needs clearing. I just mean that I found a place to start moving to being lighter. I have also then been able to work towards healing and forgiving myself as well.

Actually, forgiving becomes a word that is irrelevant as it becomes... "it just is". And they did what they did knowing what they knew, with the skills they had. My parents both had very hard up childhoods and developed their life skills based on their experiences and observations. I do look differently at my dad who, later when I was a teen, would go to church and sit in judgement of others then come home and do what he did there. Some things were in total contradiction to what we had just been taught was right. But here again I chose him as my father, perhaps to learn from him and to choose differently for my children...

I have learnt to be in service of others and how to enjoy whatever task you have to do at this moment. I was taught to be available to others in perceived need, and even to perceive their needs before they needed to voice them.

I thank both of my parents, as well as grandparents, for the lessons I have learnt as we have travelled this path. As I sit here typing I ask that all who have felt judged, or measured by me, that you will understand and forgive me and accept that I am still learning... as are we all. That together we can move through the remainder of this time together working towards a space of non-judgement and acceptance of all we meet in life.

This doesn't mean you have to tolerate my bad behaviour, or violence to self, but that we are all walking in awareness. We can move away from environments before these things can occur, or simply recognise, and not allow those people to be in our space. As we live more consciously, we can move away, as did the wild animals of East Africa and Indonesia, as the tidal waves approached their lands. It was only the unconscious human and domestic animals that perished.

Many times, we only remember only the "Good" or, only the "Bad". In truth, life is about both and, sometimes, even filled with so-so stuff that just passes us by un-noticed. All these things touch us and influence us, and how we interact with the world.

WHO AM I?

Have you ever watched the musical "Les Miserables"? There is a song in the show where Val Jean sings.... "Who am I?" What a song! What a question to ask ourselves! As he asks this question, he is also brutally honest to himself with his answers. There are things that we retrospectively ask of ourselves as we go through life, as we try to come to terms with what we perceive as... "Our Life" and who we think we are, even of what we are.

To those who share my indigenous ancestry, I am of the four winds. I whakapapa to the Tail (Nga Puhi), to both the left (Kahungungu), and the right wings (Ngati Awa) as well as to the main body, of the fish (Raukawa, Tuwharetoa and Ngati Pikiau). Because of what I saw growing up in Raetihi my Maunga (mountain) is Ruapehu and my Awa (river) is Te Whanganui. For those of the rest of the world I am also of the four winds, in that I am of Irish, Yorkshire, Norwegian, and New Zealand Maori descent.

Well, where to start. I have had so many people tell me I need to write this down so others can see there is hope. And to be truthful I have started several times over the years but didn't like what I read and wrote about myself. I don't want to come across as poor "Me" or "I'm special", as this very is far from the truth. We are all unique and all have a special journey to "Be" and "Enjoy" before we are complete here.

I have always believed there is more to this life than... "be born, live, drop dead and cease to exist." I guess it has been that inner knowing that has kept me going most of my life. You know...that little voice in the head (and not so little sometimes, when it was important) that whispers... "Don't do that!" or "Don't go there", or as happened once when I was fifteen, and about drive off on an errand, a very loud... "Gregory! Put your seatbelt on" sounded in my mind. I didn't make it to the shop, and the car I was driving was written off in the accident when a hit and run driver ploughed into the side of the car. Needless to say, I have learnt to trust these little promptings. So, you can say I have always had my own proof of another existence.

Let's just talk here about this knowing and more for a moment before I start on the story of me...

A few years ago, while struggling with yet another relationship coming to a close, my partner had decided to get a Psychic and her friend to come and work on her. She also decided that I could also use some help. Of course, I agreed to this. During my session, with the Psychic lady, we talked about many things including my tupuna (ancestors etc and our connection) and my 4 near-death (out of body) experiences. She reminded me that it was no wonder I was unhappy here, as I could still remember what if felt like to be out my body and free. I don't talk about this much as many times people scoff and tell me its wasn't real! Just my imagining! It seemed the more I heard this the more I shut the hell up.

Well, no matter what these fearful and judgemental people say, for me it is real! Very real! Since this time, I have heard others describe very similar space, energy and even events leading to their choosing to return to the body and heal themselves... Anita Moorjani wrote her book "Dying to live". A friend of mine who had been sceptical of my story saw an interview she did with Dr. Wayne Dyer. Afterwards my friend looked at me differently and said... "She (Anita Moorjani) describes it just like you do."

So here goes *(in brief... very brief)*

WHAT DRIVES ME…

The first 3 times I left my body were so amazing. There are really no words to describe the sense of being, or the sense of joy and gratitude you feel *(for want of a better word because you don't actually feel anything! It's simply Awareness)*. There is no pain!!! There was no heaviness!! There is no judgement, just welcoming and gratitude and allowance. Each time I became aware of others near me, first just colours and energy… Then slowly I was aware of form. I was also aware of the joy I had within as I moved at speed of thought to some I knew and recognised. At this point, I would "hear" … "What are you doing here?" "You must go back… you must go back now!" I'm saying no!! I don't want to…! (I had my reasons) and after a brief discussion I would be back in my body with tears on my face. The hardest for me was I still felt and remembered that space. That energy. That joy. I was angry each time a friend died and I wasn't allowed to. It was so unfair… Eventually I let go and simply accepted that I can't die. With this… I lost all fear, as even if I died it doesn't mean the end *(for me it would simply mean a new beginning to embrace)*. This made flying easy. Coming into Wellington Airport during a storm was almost exciting as it became a fun roller coaster ride for me. My partner was a little put out with my lack of empathy for her and other passengers...

The fourth time I left my body was different. The universe (it seems) decided someone needed to have a word with Greg, face to face so to speak...

A bee from a passing swarm stung me under my fourth toe on my left foot. Within 20 minutes I was paralysed and unable to move or speak. I could not make a sound. On the funny side... Have you ever tried to blink loud enough to get someone's attention? It can't be done. I know! I tried several times. Admittedly, they were kind of slow... but very deliberate.

All I will say is that when I gained conscious awareness of self and body, I was calm. Incredibly calm and peaceful. I knew I had a job to complete. I knew it is important. This knowing has pushed me hard to make choices that have been hard, and even hurtful to others, when viewed from the outside. I still remember the space and I still miss it... but differently. I know I can create and be that space anytime I choose. I do "create this space" each time I present a class, or work with someone and their body during a session.

So where is this all leading to?

Gregory D Bryers MSc.

Have you ever held a new baby? I mean "really" held the baby and been totally present with it. Have you looked in to its eyes and said… "hello"? What is it about this baby that makes this moment so special? What is it you become (Consciously or unconsciously) aware of? Some people describe it as a taste of heaven. For me I describe it as a sense of total trust and peace. The essence of real unconditional love. No judgement!! Somewhere between that moment and when they grow up…they loose this space, "We" lost this space.

I'm here to show you that it is not lost. Just hidden. As we made ourselves "less than" so we could fit into this crazy reality called life. We are told we are dreamers or too much or too loud or! Or! Or!

I'm here to remind you of who you really are and how you can recreate you and more if you would only choose to be you…whoever you decide you are, at any given moment in time…And for crying out loud stop trying to find the "authentic" you!! What a load of proverbial crap, designed to keep you searching and relying on some asshole to keep telling you are nearly there. You are "there" and always have been. You are just under the rubble everyone loaded on you as you grew up. All those comments, judgements, expectations, projections about who and what you are (what they want you to be). This is all to limit and define you. I'm here to invite you to be undefinable. Are you willing to be all things without significance? Here is an example... Me! Petit Moi!

Definitions and labels of me... Koro (grandad) Egg, Grandad, Opa, magic hands, healer, teacher, husband, father, friend, bastard (yup some peeps don't like me), business competitor, student of 60 years, home handy man, walking miracle... blah blah. Which one of these is actually me? These are all roles I play when required, but they don't define who I am, because the infinite part of me has been all things *(and still can be)*.

How many times are we taught to look to others for the way to find us? We are taught to look outside ourselves to find happiness, joy, purpose, and even who we think we are *(or should be)*. I'm here to remind you to look within to that still space that is you. There you will find that you create all these things for you. They don't come from outside...you create them ... you choose to be them. Everyday till you no longer need to choose because you already are them.

So back to the story....

WHOOPS!

In 1993, while studying at the University of Waikato (as a mature student – what a label), I experienced what we thought had been my first stroke (can someone remind me to explain later). During the whole experience I felt an amazing calm come over me. Even though I couldn't communicate with my friends, as they tried to keep me awake and breathing (you know all the things we think of as important at the time someone is having a bad day), I was calm within. I felt almost as an observer. I also knew very clearly that I had had a stroke. I couldn't feel my left arm, speech was slurred and then something in my mouth got in the way and I couldn't speak. Everything came out wrong. A friend, trying to keep me alert, commented on how lucky I was, as the last time he got legless and couldn't talk, it had cost him a fortune and I had got there for free. I still get a grin when I think of that day and the way my friends worked to distract and keep me conscious.

The campus doctor came along saying that I was... "Fine, and just hyperventilated". He hadn't done any of the checks he had recently taught the graduates to do when first aiding students in distress. So the ambulance staff walked me to the lift... my left leg now dragging. Down to the ground floor and out to the ambulance. As I was such a large fellow (125+ kg) they, in their wisdom, decided that I would have to get myself into the back. I did and off we went to the university medical centre where we repeated the procedure, in reverse...except that as we "strolled" into the building, my left leg said no!! Short story of the moment is everyone cleared the ways as I went down and then they helped me up. By the time I was in the surgery room (doctors consult room) my face was getting very numb and left side had dropped even more. A lovely nurse took one look, spoke the word "bugger" rushed out and back again with the doctor in tow. He then said something under his breath, and off to the hospital we went.

I can remember sitting on a gurney bed (you know... one of those really uncomfortable hospital beds they use in the emergency rooms) oblivious to anything and wondering why I was sharing my room with a lady and her little boy. The doctors kept asking if I had seen my wife and I started getting upset as I hadn't. I couldn't even tell them what she looked like, her name, or even my name... silly when you look back as they kept calling me Mr Bryers (I should have known my first name was mister aye). I have another clear memory of them telling this lady that... "He was fine" and that "He just has a migraine." This lady then said... "Well we're off on holiday so he can have some rest while we're away." Still no connection to who she was even though I was, by coincidence, taking my family away the next day as well. The doctor then told her ... "He (I now understand was Me) would be in hospital for at least three to six months." Of course, you can imagine the look on this lady's face when she said, ... "For a migraine?"

I still don't remember when I made the connection to the lady sharing my cubicle, but at some point, I realised she was Joy, my wife and the little boy was Michael, my youngest son. One thing that kept coming to me over the following weeks and months, was how grateful I was that it had happened the day it did, and not while I was driving the vehicle with my precious load in the car.

Well, to cut a long story short, after three episodes and having my butt planted into a wheelchair, I became quite depressed. I was at a rehab unit when the staff suggested that I have dinner with a friend. They organised it and off I went. Young Karen is an amazing person and one of my greatest inspirations. This young lady had been in one of my first-year class's at University (Biology 101a) but disappeared sometime during that first semester. She had a car accident and broke C1 (at the base of her skull). Wasn't supposed to be able to breathe un-aided, let alone live in a flat with her dog. I have sat in my wheelchair (in awe of this amazing young lady) and pushed her wheelchair while she walked twenty-one metres around the rehab gym using a walking frame. Karen gave me the determination, and courage, to keep moving, to keep living, and to live my life more joyfully. I thank her for her amazing example of courage and determination.

My four children (Benjamin, Megan, Lara, and Michael) have also been such an inspiration, and help, to me. I don't remember feeling any judgement, or displeasure, from them as I worked to overcome weakness and my inability to function as "normal". My daughters would encourage me to sing with them, to help me practice speech and making clear sounds. I recently watched an old video of me back then. I was talking to a visitor at our home and my two youngest were busy using me as a jungle gym or climbing wall. They show no fear and total trust in me and that I will catch them. It was a hard time for them all as they were unsure as to whether dad would be home, at hospital or even alive, when they got home from school each day.

At the time it was a bone of contention, as well as source of perceived stress, but my eldest son had a delivery run. He delivered pamphlets to letterboxes around our neighbourhood. I would spend the day folding and sorting into bundles. I made myself do this, where ever and when ever possible, using my left hand to do the bulk of the work. This was extremely tiring and at times, and I would simply pass out and sleep at the table while doing the job. At first, these sleeps would be quite frequent but as time progressed, and I got more able, they became less needed and I became more agile and co-ordinated with my left side. At one point I noticed I was becoming very left handed. Twenty years down the line and I can still be driving my car and realise that my left hand has been planted on my lap, un-used. I would then make my hand participate in the driving process and hold the steering wheel. I have realised that I still need to function in a very conscious fashion and, that as I do this, my body then also functions well and fully. We become trapped in habit of movement and use of our limbs. Consciously using my legs and noting how my feet sound as I walk allows me to hear and notice any imbalances in my stride. I have found this to be true of even the most able-bodied people that come to me for therapy. We get to a level of non-thinking about our body and function from habit and very unconsciously. As they become more body aware and become more conscious, they are also noticing that they move more fluidly. Often, they comment on feeling less restrictions etc. One client I have had the pleasure of working with over a long period of time has always had an amazing range of motion in his upper body. Surprising considering his profession, that of a Diesel Mechanic working on big trucks etc. He commented that he treated his work as his gym and would stretch through any restrictions he would feel. But his back pain wouldn't go away until we began addressing the restrictions and imbalances in his lower back and legs. I recently watched him perform on stage with a group of friends and noticed that he, although being probably one of the oldest there, was the most agile and relaxed in his movements. There is a great deal to be said for being, and moving more consciously, through everyday life.

In my journey towards wellness I have had to make some really hard realisations about me, and about life. I have had a lot of input from people who cared, as well as from people who didn't, and it has been part of that journey to discover how to tell the difference. Some well meaning, others just mean, but that's another journey and another story. As part of my recovery, a lady I knew as Aunty Rangi, offered to come and massage me on a weekly basis. This was both amazing and painful, but exciting at the same time. It seemed to reconnect the dots, so to speak, and reminded the brain that there was indeed a left side. We also found that my right side was extra sensitive and compensating for the lack of feeling in the left. This wonderful lady also put me on the path of a journey to self-discovery and understanding that will last till, and beyond, my last breath. Her love and patience with me will live on as I pay it forward to others with whom I have the honour and pleasure to work with, and for.

A really good friend (Morgan) had just completed his training in rehabilitation and physio care came to visit. I thought that I was doing really well in recovery but was shocked to discover how far I still had to go. He took me through a couple of tests, which demonstrated to me what was ahead. Morgan showed me a set of exercises to do and these I did, almost to distraction. Simple one's, like putting my hand out in front and taking from prone (palm down) to supine (palm up). Yes, I could do that one (with my eyes open) but when I shut my eyes, I ceased to "feel" my arm and hand and so couldn't tell if it was moving, or not, let alone if it was up or down facing. It actually caused a deep feeling of panic and fear, the first time I tried this exercise.

It's interesting here…I find as a therapist I now do the opposite and look away from what it is I'm massaging so that I can gain a better perception of what it is my hands are aware of within the tissue. When teaching massage, I would ask a student what they feel and they would immediately look with their eyes, thus turning off their "perception" and "feel". As I got them to turn their sight off and perceive more with their hands and being, they in turn could go deeper into the massage without force.

I also tried a number of tried and true methods for improving my memory. Pieces of paper didn't work, as I forgot I even had the piece of paper, and so resorted to writing on the back of my hand. This worked as long as I didn't wash my hands too thoroughly. Pieces of string didn't work as one, I couldn't put it on the hand that had feeling and two, if I put it on the hand that had no feeling then I for-

That Book!

got it was there...and then forgot what the string was for. I had to carry my student ID with me everywhere, as when people asked me my name, even if they said ... "Hey Greg, what's your name?" I didn't have a clue. An example of this was one day my wife asked me to go into a bank in town and cash a cheque for her. I was stressed and tired but did as requested. As I walked up to the teller, I realised that I didn't know her, as I was unfamiliar with this branch, and suddenly I started to panic. The teller asked me if this was my cheque and I could only reply that I thought so. She then asked me my name...and there she had me. I didn't know. Fortunately, a staff member from the branch I normally go, was there and, came to my rescue. After reassuring the teller that I was actually the person named in the cheque, and that she knew me, I was given the money and sent on my way. It took me a long time before I would go to unfamiliar shops etc after that. At campus I would only deal with department staff with whom I was familiar. Friends with whom I had studied with for the past 3 and half years were so patient and kind. They soon worked out that if I hadn't spoken to, or seen them, in the past couple of months then there was a huge chance I would know that I knew them, but would not know their names. This I found very distressing, and even after nearly twenty years passing it is still my biggest hurdle to overcome.

Is any of the above familiar? I'm sure that if you have

had a stroke or even head injury you will be able to relate to at least part of what I have said. Those of you who have family, or friends, that have been affected by strokes may also "see" similar situations with your friends and loved ones. The reason for the above stories is to just show that we all have similar issues and some will vary to different extremes. You are normal and I would like to tell you that they can be overcome and things re-gathered back into the whole of who you are...what ever you see, or perceive, as you. You can recover to being fully normal or part thereof. It really just depends on you, and what you are prepared to do to get there. I have had clients who have achieved results to various levels of recovery and stopped. Why? Because they had done what they wanted to do and didn't want to put any more effort into moving further along. They are content with where they are, and I just had to learn to accept that. And I do, and love them for the lessons I have learned from them, about me, and the way I BE.

SIGNPOSTS TO A DIFFERENT PATH…

There are many Angels that walk among us and touch our lives in some way, or another, to help move us in a direction that will help and heal us. Some come and go un-noticed with quiet words of wisdom while others arrive with a big stick when we are being stubborn or reluctant. Some have touched my life simply by their example of endurance and just being, while others have touched me from afar and we have never met.

One such "Angel" that walked among us is called Louise Hay. This lady is loved and respected the world over. She has worked with a wide range of people in helping them to overcome horrific affliction and prejudice because of health and /or life styles. A book she wrote called "You can Heal your Life" has had a profound effect on me. First it made me very angry…then just plain grumpy and then finally remorseful at my reaction to a deep truth.

In her book she identifies thoughts and beliefs of, and about, ourselves that help us create the illness slash dis-ease that brings us to a juncture in our universe. So, when I looked up strokes, I got hit in the face with a huge cast iron frying pan. Louise pointed out that strokes are about... *"Giving up". "Resistance" and ... "I'd rather die than change." "A rejection of Life!"* Rather to the point aye. Myself being in denial and angry thought ... *"No way! I want to live! Who is this woman and what would she know anyway?"* But as time allowed her gentle words to slowly seep deeper into the grey cell that rattled alone inside the cranial bones, I call my head, I realised how true those words were and still are today. When a client comes in and asks if I can help a family member who has had a stroke these words come back to me and so I ask the hard question of the family member who has had the stroke. "When did you decide to Die?" and always they look at me and acknowledge the point. At this point, I then ask "Do you still want to die, or have you changed your mind?" If they take their time sorting out the answer, I usually find that even if they say they want to live, they actually "don't", and that is ok because that is where they are at, at this point in their lives. And anyway...who am I to judge what is right and what is wrong for them. Have I walked where they have walked? My perspective on life has changed because someone asked me the hard question and had the love and understanding to not judge me for my thoughts, feelings and emotions about life and why I then found it... "too hard to keep on keeping on!"

Thankfully while at University of Waikato I was introduced to a bloke prepared to ask the hard question of me, (He was a counsellor in the student health centre there on campus and no I can't remember his name sorry) and then point out that ... *"If you die Greg, your kids won't have a dad..."* This pulled me up short, and helped me to claim life and make changes... whatever that required.

Over the next few years many things happened and I let go many things that I held as important, unchangeable, and even sacred to my way of being. I re-read Louise Hay several times, Wayne Dyer, Ekhart Tolle, and many other inspirational books. I learned to meditate, still my mind, discovered Chi Gong and so on. Through all this I kept learning about me, about many of the things I still held, deep within, that reinforced that Gregory wasn't "good enough", "wasn't worthy". I also learnt that I had a great deal of trouble receiving from others. I was the best giver on the planet and would give until there was no more of Gregory to give. To receive even a compliment was difficult, and if someone was to give me a gift, I was always looking for the draw string, or the condition, on which it was given *(unconditional love was not real in my world... even from my Grandmother...).* Wow what a head job aye. Realising that this stems back to childhood I have worked on letting this go and being able to accept gifts more readily now. That is not to say that it's easy but it's a lot easier than then. Life is about constantly moving, evolving and moving. Life is dynamic and constantly trying to achieve some form of balance and equilibrium. I guess the best-known depiction of this constant striving is the yin yang logo of many eastern martial arts groups.

Many things have happened since the time of my first stroke and completing my studies at the University of Waikato. I Graduated with a Masters in Science and technology (with honours) and then completed a diploma in Geography before moving to Wellington (NZ) and studying Massage at the New Zealand School of Massage. This was an interesting space to be in. To get to class I would have to leave my wheelchair in the car and negotiate three flights of stairs. There I would stay until the end of the day and then would make my way downstairs again. Initially this would take around ten minutes each way. By the time I graduated (18 months later) I could grab my bag and run up the stairs and go straight into class.

I am so grateful to the Directors and tutors of the college for their faith and trust in me. Being able to study and continue on until completion of the course. This set of classes and study program allowed me to reconnect with my body, to realise that I could move forward and let go my disability. I learned to let go of stress that would have normally left me unable to clearly communicate or function. I could sit exams and clearly and easily function (eventually- by the end of my diploma). My tutors have been very supportive and loving.

One tutor was my cousin Trudi. She showed me how to move through this world in a very clear and loving manner. Even while struggling with cancer and relationship changes etc she was peaceful and loving to those she taught. She is an inspiration, and someone who will walk with me in the fields of my mind until we meet again in person. I often hear her laughter ringing in my ears as I struggle with something. Usually something, that if I was truly honest, I could have left alone and it would have sorted itself out, without the fuss, or the bother, I created around it. Trudi was my first real introduction to the question… "What else is possible?" This is something I will talk about later…Would someone please remind me.

I am grateful to all the people who have aided me in my recovery by not trying to restrict me, but to encourage, support, and even push, me to move outside my comfort zone. Some, by their amazing examples of courage, strength, and love, and as such, are shining lights in my life. Others by bringing new possibilities and ideas on how I can "Move" and "Be" in this world. By allowing me to be me. I thank you.

WHAT IS THE DREAM YOU HAVE GIVEN UP ON IN LIFE?

"It's what you have always wanted to accomplish. Everyone, when they are young, knows what their Personal Legend is.
At that point in their lives, everything is clear and everything is possible. They are not afraid to dream, and to yearn for everything they would like to see happen to them in their lives. But, as time passes, a mysterious force begins to convince them that it will be impossible for them to realise their Personal Legend. (Paulo Coelho, The Alchemist, 25th Anniversary Edition, 2014.)

We often read about some Guru, Avatar, or other Enlightened Traveller, and think wow, wouldn't it be awesome to be like them. What an amazing person to be like that. We often fail to realise that they often took years and years to achieve the end results that appear so miraculous to us. Paramahansa Yoganada (Autobiography of a Yogi) didn't just suddenly become "Aware". He didn't just wake up one morning and say… "Wow! I'm amazing." No! he had teachers. He had lessons, some of which were very humbling, others even painful. But what he did have, was a dream and a knowing to which he held fast. He knew he wanted to be like the Yogi's he had met. He knew he had a Teacher waiting to teach him, and he kept searching and striving to fulfil that dream. So here is a question for you to ponder… and no, you don't need to tell me the answer. "What is the dream you have given up… to be what you feel other people expect you to be?"

To put it another way… "What unconsciousness are you using to invalidate you, and your awareness, in order to validate others, their judgements, and conclusions, about how you should be?"

Man, the first time I got asked that question it really hit home. I thank a very dear friend for having the love to ask it of me. How many times have you put your dreams on hold, or given them up permanently in order to "Keep the peace"? Many clients that I have asked these questions of have forgotten the dreams and aspirations of their youth. It has been so long since they have allowed themselves to have a dream, or desire, that they cannot remember any of the old dreams. And sadly, they have forgotten how to create new dreams to move towards.

What would happen if we stopped giving ourselves up for others? What would happen if we started choosing and creating for ourselves and became the invitation for people who actually like us (yes I say "like us", not like who they think we should be) to come join us on a different journey of discovery and creation?

I have forgotten how many times I have read and then re-read "The Alchemist" by Paulo Coehlo **(*The Alchemist*, Paulo Coehlo, 25th Aniversary edition, 2014)**. I find it fascinating and very educational in understanding what I see from my life and reality. In chapter 10 the King of Salem is talking to the boy about this very stuff. Where people give up their personal dream (*called "your Personal Legend" in the book...*) because something convinces them it will be impossible, or we decide other things must be more important. We put off dreams to get married, or to please a partner, a parent, or, or, or to simply keep the peace at home.

At some very deep level they become impoverished, and are functioning from a non-participatory state. In this state you cannot possibly achieve "wellness", as you cannot dream of being whole, happy, and able bodied. If you don't allow yourself to hold onto a dream, then you won't allow anything like a dream to come to fruition.

"What do you want to do, when you get well?"
"Where would you like to go when you get well?"
"If you could change something in your life Who would you like to be?"
"What would it take to be truly "You"?"
…Go on… "Live in the question!" and then prepare for phenomenal life, and the changes that come from changing your mind.

In his book Spiritually Incorrect Enlightenment (2010) pg. 95, Jed McKenna, *says… "If Curtis really wants this, it will really occur, but the kind of wanting required is the kind that starts in the Mind and moves to the Heart and then reaches out from the centre. It takes time and it can be as much a pull toward one thing as a push from another."*

How many times do we say we desire something, but, in our mind, we have created reasons why we can't have it? And we isolate that desire so that we don't feed it, water it, or let it grow to fruition? We shut our heart down so we can't possibly choose, or desire it… because it's not possible. In a recent class a young lady declared she had been asking for something but it just didn't show up! And she then asked me why it hasn't if all we have to do is imagine it and create it and then be it. My reply was simple… She hadn't really chosen it! Yes! I have! She declared. So, I asked what was her thought immediately after her asking the universe (herself really) for the thing she was asking for? She said "nothing" but everyone in the class also felt it... and then she finally said... "It is not possible..."

She was already negating the request, and so like many others I suggested she let go the last negative thought and only see it as already there. A short while later she put a post on Facebook that she was on her way to live in Norway and work at her dream job, made possible because she stopped telling the universe it was not possible. Where are you creating hurdles and insurmountable obstacles to prevent you from having all you desire ...like good health and wellness?

What do you think would be possible if, when we truly desire something with our mind, and we let go the stories about what is possible and not, and then we feel with our heart the joy of actually being and receiving the desire? To actually see it actualize, and to become real in our minds, and then feel it become real with our heart, and then with every cell and molecule of our body to the point where we radiate the energy of actually being and having what it is that we desire!

How would this be for you? How could we then affect our body? Our Health? Our way of Being? It got me, and my big ass, out of my wheelchair....so what could you change... if you really chose it?

When did you stop creating from your dreams and desires and knowing all things were possible? Would you choose now to change that and begin again...?

NEVER GIVE UP!!

People I would meet would tell me that they thought I was amazing. You know...being in a wheelchair then walking, and working, and doing so called "normal" things, and not giving up.

The truth is that I gave up many times. Not on life, but sometimes I got tired and gave up on trying. I never once stopped seeing myself normal, or not walking, but there were times when I felt so bone tired that it was easier to just not try anymore, and in the end, I just let go. I let go of life, of living, of everything that I perceived as important in my universe.

But guess what... "You guessed it!" Yes, "my" universe would send someone along, who just knew what to say, or do, to inject caring back into my vocabulary, back into my being. If that didn't work, I usually got my backside kicked to get me moving again. Often the softest word had the greatest impact.

While studying at university someone emailed me a picture titled "Don't ever give up!" It shows a stork with his mouth over the head of a frog. The frog has

That Book!

his arms out the sides of the bird's mouth and his hands tightly squeezing the bird's throat. This has kept me moving forward also in my life.

Don't ever give up!

Sadly, it seems that our human-ness leads us to

the very brink of destruction before we wake up and realise where we are, and to make the required changes. Then of course this may happen several times over several cycles, as we get better, then forget the changes and slip back into habits and unconscious patterns, and then make changes again. Its not until we make these changes permanent that the most profound changes happen and true healing takes place. It's taken me a while...! And I am still working towards more of whatever it is... if that is even real anymore...

I didn't get better over night. It took lots of falls, struggles and frustrating moments to get improvement after improvement. It was really easy to complain that things were going too slowly, but friends would then point out how far I had come and encourage me to keep moving onward and upward. You may find it hard to identify improvements, in your self, while they happen, as you are with them all the time and so don't see the subtle shifts in energy levels, abilities to focus on tasks, speech and so many other aspects of daily life. However, friends, who may not see you as often as we would like, see them and can remind us of where we were and where we are now. They are one of the most valuable things you have...apart from the ability to keep breathing.

Oh yes, and wasn't it exquisite the first time you were able to feed yourself in public without embarrassing anyone. As I have made my steps towards recovery, I have also learnt that the most important things in life aren't "Things", they are those people around me who honour me, and in so doing allow me to honour them, and most importantly myself. They trust me and allow me to trust and feel trusted. They recognise my vulnerability and allow me to be vulnerable, as I work through my stuff. They are in allowance of my weakness and shortfalls and express their gratitude for the things they see in me that I don't quite see for myself. They also allow me to express my gratitude for all that I am and can be without judgement, or condition. These people have been able to show and express an intimacy and love that is deeply nurturing and again I say thank you, thank you, thank you.

It is so important to surround yourself with loving uplifting people. I said loving and uplifting, not sympathetic and coddling. You have to be "allowed" to "do and be" or you will collapse under your own rubble of self-destruction, as your sense of dis-empowerment and dependence on those around you overwhelms you. Or,

you could just get lazy, and get everyone running around after you until they can't be bothered anymore. Then you are on your own having to learn without help to do the things you should have been learning to do in the first place. I made lots of mistakes, had lots of falls, forgot more than I remembered, but I kept moving forward with my dream of walking normally and being "Normal" (if there really is such a thing) or being alive.

Normal! Ha! Only a scientist with arrogance of a billy goat would coin such a phrase. *While I'm being grumpy, I developed a particular dislike for the word and title of INVALID. People would ask if I had my invalid sticker, or did I park in the invalid park etc. tell me what the difference between an invalid person, and an invalid licence is? The spelling is the same but we just pronounce it differently. Does that mean that while I was dis-abled, I was also INVALID. But I digress and ranting isn't pretty aye. Words and how we use them, and how they can be mis-applied.*

GLASS HALF FULL OR HALF EMPTY

Have you ever noticed how some people, no matter how much they have in their glass it is always empty and yet to others their glass has enough... for now. Some are always looking to get more from everyone (as they function from a space of lack or the world owes me) and others are content knowing more is possible should they choose it. That doesn't mean they won't say yes to more but there is enough for now in their glass. Where is yours? Are you a taker or a receiver? What do I mean by that? Just that! Do you take everything from anyone because its offered and because you have the right to do so, or do you receive from people because again it is offered and you are grateful for the offering, and the "gifting". You know that even people who are "paid" to do the job of caring for you are gifting to you their energy, their love, and their time. They don't have to and if you are ungrateful and don't acknowledge that this is true then what tends to happens is that you go through a lot of home help, a lot of care givers, and a lot of friends. When you receive and acknowledge the gifting with gratitude, thankfulness, and joy, people tend to go the extra mile for you. They are there for you in so many more ways than you could possibly imagine.

I love how Dr Wayne Dyer puts it in his talk "Wishes fulfilled" which you can view on YouTube.com by the way. He says we can wake up in the morning and go… "Good God! Morning!" or we can say… "Good morning God!"

How we live life is a choice. Abraham (Esther Hicks) puts it this way… "Life! How you view (*and live*) it is optional! It's totally up to you.

GRATITUDE...

On one of those many occasions I ended up at the Waikato Hospital and was under close observation (you know...those two hourly blood pressure checks, is he breathing? ...Responsive? type schedules) and it was two am and the nurse came to check in on me. Her first words to me were... "How do you do that Greg?" As I couldn't speak, I wrote... "What?" She replied that as she came in and before my eyes had opened, my mouth was already smiling. My reply was simple... "I woke up!" At that time, each time I went to sleep I was never sure I would wake in the morning. This is something we take for granted and accept as always going to happen, and so have no gratitude for it when it happens. I am grateful for all that I have, for the well-being that I enjoy, for the chance to make changes in my life, and to further improve how I am, and even Who I am. To be able to watch others make similar changes and witness the improvements to their health and well-being is phenomenal to say the least. It feeds my being and fills my body with Joy.

This was something I read and had read to me by a teacher when I was 14 years old. It rang in my universe like a gong and a call to strive for more. I decided that this I would like to feel I have accomplished and succeeded at before I am walking among the stars again. It's a quote used by Ralph Waldo Emerson and the words put it really well

... *"To laugh often and much; To win the respect of intelligent people and the affection of children; To earn the appreciation of honest critics and endure the betrayal of false friends; To appreciate beauty, to find the best in others; To leave the world a bit better, whether by a healthy child, a garden patch, or a redeemed social condition; To know even one life has breathed easier because you have lived. This is to have succeeded."* **Ralph Waldo Emerson (1803 - 1882) American Essayist & Poet**

So again I will ask more questions.
"Are you living your bliss?"
"Are you being you?"
"Are you living your dream?"

So, what would it take for everything to fall into place, and for you to start living? How would that feel? What was the dream you have denied yourself, in order to fit into society, your social group, rugby club, church circles?

While I was studying at university, I presented a paper in geography on social pressures put on by peer groups and family. Education and people. *This paper had a particular orientation to Maori people because that is who I truly identified with…my people. I'm also Irish etc, but this is where I stand, on the Whenua*

(Land). In the paper, I was able to identify a key issue with Maori moving forward in this world. The parents have to stop crushing the dreams of their children. I used the example of Dr Paewai. This man was originally from Dannevirke and grew up working with the family shearing and working the farms but wanted to be a medical doctor. The story goes that he was told and reminded that he was getting above himself... not by the European segment in the community but by his own family. His mother failed to support him, and so sadly he took himself away from them, to follow his dream. Long story cut short, he became one of Northland's most known and respected. The people of the far north cherished him for the Taonga (gift) that he was to the land and its people. He never gave up on his dream.

So, what dream have you given up on? I'm still asking this one of me too by the way. What stupidity am I using to invalidate my reality in order to validate other people's realities? What is it I have given up so that others feel comfortable around me? So that others will feel important, even feel loved? We are taught to love others, before ourselves, or we are being selfish. If we are running around for others to the detriment of self, to the point of collapse, are we honouring them? Are we really? Now they have to choose whether they will stick with a cripple (become a martyr) or move on (and become a failure and someone who walked out when the other needed them most). What a head job aye. In a discussion on this subject I told my wife back then that... "if I was too hard then I will find a flat." Her reply was actually quite saddening to me... "I'm in this for the long haul." Wow so I was just a burden to be carried. Not likely.

Needless to say, I got a flat... then actually left town and moved to another city. I let go of all those things that had been important to me. I started to look at what was real and true for me, and discovered that there wasn't as much as I had previously decided was actually true and real. It had been decided that because I was (in the words of my childrens mum) "a big man" that I could hurt my children, that I could only visit my children under supervision. This happened only once.

A cousin of mine was asked to be the chaperone, so to speak, and she agreed. It was uncomfortable and I really felt ashamed that anyone would give me a label of such that I needed supervision with my own children, while still allowing my abusive father open visiting privileges to them. *(This I realise still sticks me as the children's mother knew his history with me, and my sisters)*. At the end of the very strained visit I wrote to the courts and told them that I would not be put in such a position again. That it was unkind to myself and to my children, and so my children were welcome to come visit whenever they chose, and that I would await their requests. It took five very long years... and then my youngest daughter, much to her siblings horror requested to come visit. I still celebrate her courage, and her determination, and I am deeply grateful for her love. To cut a long and very boring story short, we (my four children and 7 grandchildren) even have a fun and kind rapport.

I spoke of things that I let go of... One of these "things" was any significance I had around my children. I would no longer be held captive, nor controlled, because of my desire to see, or be with my children. This was not easy and I went through a long grieving process around this. I also let go of any significance I had with what I thought a family meant...siblings, aunties, uncles, parents etc.

The hardest was that connection with my Mum. Little boys always want their mums, and I was no exception *(even at nearly 60)*. I used to endure a lot of pain due to being caught with letters I had written to my mum. They didn't get posted, as I was too young to know how, or have the money for the stamps. As an adult, I got to reconnect with Mum but it seemed that there were always conditions, and finally I also realised how much pain it caused her when we got together, and so have even let that go now. The last time I was in my mum's presence all I wanted was to be touched and held by her but that wasn't going to happen. Sadly, the pain I felt from her was just that... and then I realised that I was a cause of that pain and discomfort. I simply let go, and in my mind promised her I would not willingly be the cause of more for her. I cannot, and will not, judge her for her choices, as I have not walked in her shoes. I can choose to honour her for the courage and strength it took to walk away, so that our father didn't kill her, as he had promised he would.

I also let go many other things. Things I had always seen as Good, Bad, and, or Ugly etc, I became indifferent to in many ways. They became just "things" as I became more in allowance and less judgemental of them. That doesn't mean I won't stop someone beating or abusing a child, or a woman, but I see a different picture now.

So, as they say...

"Now what?"

Well I have trained as a builder, a scientist, as a massage therapist and more. What can I add to people's lives that will create ease and more joy for them? What can I add to my own life to create more ease and joy in my life? I guess I am required to work on me first, and then I can be the invitation to more for others. This is what I have been working at for some time.

Something I have learned on the way...I'm a healer. This doesn't mean I come along and touch and wam!! I take your illness away. Nope, not even. I have watched healers die as a result of doing just that. Taking peoples stuff into their own bodies in order to heal someone. Husbands, wives, siblings, and children, all taking pain and stuff from the one they care about, to the point of illness for themselves, only to see the one they care so deeply for get worse, or die anyway. I have learned to not take it on board. I learned to recognise much of what I felt as not mine, and not own it, or try to make it fit into my reality.

This awareness has helped me to acknowledge what it is I perceive as belonging to others...usually the one I am working with. I also have realised that as I started developing a clinic etc I consciously set up my room as a space for healing. A space where people could come and not feel judged by what they felt, said, believe they have done, or even what their body may, or may not, look like. By consciously creating and holding that space I have also created it as a way of being. Sure, there are times when I slip, and get human, and say or do things that may upset someone. I'm still learning too, and have upset friends. This has also caused me sadness and pain (so to speak) as I work on not repeating the error. So, I am a healer of my "self".

What if we are all healers? What if we actually heal ourselves? I know that no matter what I do for someone, if they don't choose to actually get better, they don't! Its been shown many times that diabetes can be reversed simply through diet. There is a DVD called "Simply Raw". An amazing documentary on people, and choices. You actually see those that chose to change and get well, and those that chose anti-change. You can lead a horse to water but you can't make it drink…is so true. I get so excited when I see people really choose to change and be well. They really embrace the choice and do the things that will give them freedom with their body.

So… "Are you a Healer?" would you now like to destroy, uncreate and forget everything you know about healing and being a healer? That's all your conclusions, interesting points of view, projections, and expectations that you have around this concept of being a healer, and what a healer should, or should not be. Just let them all go. And now start afresh!

What if healing wasn't about diving in, telling the body its broken, what's wrong with it, and how you single handedly are the only being on the planet that can "fix" it…?

What if it actually was more a case of acknowledging the body's own knowing and awareness? Acknowledging the body is dealing with something, and has been trying to get your (the occupant) attention, by creating some form of intensity or dis-ease (we call it pain) in the body. Then simply providing the space for the body to be "Heard" and "Acknowledged" so that you (the occupant) can start to make changes in the way it lives and allow the body to heal… sometimes instantly, as it lets go of the issue around the dis-ease.

What if simply teaching the person to actually love their body, instead of beating it into submission, or abusing it, because they didn't see themselves as desirable or good looking (from their judgemental perspective) is all that is often required to create and generate the healing?

Judgement creates contraction, restriction, limitation, and stops our perceived ability to choose. We still have choice, we just don't see it in our judgement filled, no choice world. Fear dis-empowers… we give our power away… when we no longer fear we become powerful and potent.

I would now invite you to let go all the judgements

you have about you, your body, and your life. We always have such perfect vision when we look back and are somewhat blind to what's ahead of us... Why? Well, when we made choices before now, we did so from our knowing back then. When we look back from the now, we judge our choices based on what we know now. And when we look forward in time, we can only see what we know now...so stop judging you as stupid and wrong. Would you just humour me, for as long as it takes, and just acknowledge that all your choices have brought you to this moment in space, and time. It's simple really... everything you have done has created the you, you are today...and everything you choose from here on in will create a different you tomorrow...

A little while ago we had a conversation with a person in a class that Gabi (Gabriele Liesenfeld, my wife) and I were facilitating. This person had just spent two and half days telling the same story and then justifying her story with another story. Stuck and a victim. Even her voice was pathetic and yet she was busy saying how powerful she was. I got so mad at her blankness and told her I will give her money back and send her home! She went quieter and said no, that's not what she wanted. I told her to then choose! Change the story, let it go and start creating a new story or go home, before she could waste anymore of the class participants time with her weak and pathetic act. I then told her I know exactly how she feels as I have been in the same space. However, I chose to step out of that and create something different, and in choosing got my ass out of the wheelchair, got my body functioning fully, and even got to where people understand me when I speak (mostly when I speak slowly and clearly).

Something let go, as she chose to stay in the class, and not go into the wrongness of her. She also realised that she can act the story with the funding authorities, and can be her other self when she is free and creating for herself. At lunch she asked for a private session with me, during which we explored where she had learned to be a victim and thus control those around her, and where it no longer works for her. She also discovered that by being this victimhood thing, she was victimising others, also seeing how unkind that is to others she professed to love. When she came out of the session the class participants all were amazed at how her looks had changed. Softer, more joyful and even moved freely. This lady had severe chronic pain that limited her ability to move, walk any distance, and so much more. In her last message of thanks, she told Gabi how she can walk for an hour, skip, dance and even sings again... Just from letting go the story... and choosing to create something different. Something about this story. The other class participants had been getting really pissed off with her, but when she came out of the session, and they all saw the visual difference, all that disappeared and they all genuinely embraced her and included her in their space and day. They actually showed real gratitude for this amazing lady. For her courage and desire to not only be vulnerable in front of them, or be judged by them, but also for her strength in choosing something different and choosing it now...!!

Another lady, in another class, had been complaining about ongoing pain...very long term. But whenever I asked something, or suggested something, there was always a but! Even though she vowed she wanted to change this and be well, she always came back with a "but..!" To me she had already decided that it was not going to change. That nothing will change it... not even her mind. So...

I simply said "cool" and walked away to work on and with other bodies in the class. This didn't get me any special points from some in the class, and I didn't care. I decided a long time ago to help those that really want change. Really want to create something different. This lady wasn't choosing it, and so I went off to be with others that were waiting their turn. I have seen too many examples of people creating seeming miracles in their lives by simply choosing a different way of being, a different choice, a different story. This is something I am still working towards being more of. Letting go my past injuries and stories so that I can also create miracles in my life.

What if we could let go the past? Let go the stories

of our past, of our ancestors and their past, of our cultural heritage, and decided to begin a new story today. Then tomorrow, we decided to begin a new story…again… and again… and again. What would we be teaching our families, our children, and even our parents? What effect would this have on the future? On our future?

Most importantly, "What effect would this have on our bodies?" and "How would this change things for you?" I know that for me this journey has made a remarkable effect on my body and more.

SOMETHING I LEARNED ALONG THE WAY...

The Haka has often been described by Europeans as a dance. It is not. It is loud and full of energy but it is not a competition to see how loud you can shout or what funny faces you can pull. The Haka is ultimately an expression of the potent energy we all have, deep within each and every one of us. In this reality it is frowned on to express any form of potency, or strength as this is mis-identified and mis-applied as aggression. I wonder if this is why it has become such a curiosity and spectacle here, and around the world.

In Europe and many other parts of the world it is encouraged to almost flat line our emotions. In America if you are too loud or active at school, the authorities in many states can have you medicated, so as to keep you controllable. We have definitions such as ADHD, ADD and more and again we have rules whereby we are made wrong and can be medicated. As children we are taught…told…shown that we are too much and must moderate so we don't stand out, or be noticed (especially at school). What is this about? It's about creating a population that can be easily controlled.

As a boy growing up and watching many sports events, as well as cultural events and many social occasions, where a Haka was performed, I would sit in awe watching this spectacle. I would feel the energy and the joy in performing this. There is a Haka that was very well known and all sporting teams for a number of years performed this at the beginning of a game or competition. I found out this was a story about an ancestor, and it really had nothing to do with the ferociousness of the actions. This surprised me and created many questions in my head. The biggest being "so what is this really?" and I started to watch and feel more closely. The more I saw, the more I perceived it was even less about the words spoken, but more the energy of expression and potency behind the Haka that gave it purpose.

The Haka can be used to awaken energies before battle, pay tribute to a loved one who is celebrating an achievement, has just got married, or has died. The Haka will tell a story, it may tell how we are going to treat you… once we have killed you, and even how we intend to kill you…and even though we all know people we could do this to sometimes… it's not common practice anymore.

Gregory D Bryers MSc.

Are you willing to explore and look at the potency you hide within you?
Are you willing to stop looking outside of you for the things you have always known were possibly but could not find in this reality?

What could you create in your life if you allowed yourself to be these energies, when required... to create, move, and even remove things from your reality that no longer meet your requirements?

So, let's start simple, and remember the connection to the Earth, and to the Universe... *(Oh, and this is where the mind becomes a useful tool. Its not the controller of your life and universe...it's a tool that can be harnessed to create beyond everything you know is possible and into the inconceivable. Albert Einstein, Stephen Hawking, Nicola Tesla all used their minds to look at and observe questions they were asking of themselves)*

Open up your crown and base chakra. You do this with your mind reaching out into the heavens and flow energy to you and through you into the Earth. Now reach down into the earth and flow energy from the Earth through you to the Universe. This is gifting and receiving the energies in a two-way flow and you are the link to both.

Now, become conscious of this flow in your body, inviting the cells to also receive this flow and allow the energy to move with the breath...What do you become aware of in, and around your body?

Are you more aware of the sounds and the smells around you?

Do you suddenly begin find to you loose definition of where you begin, the edges of you?

Do you start to perhaps perceive the infinite being you truly are?

Now... Invite the cells and the molecules of your body to expand their awareness out to meet you! What do you perceive now...?

Are there any intensities still getting your attention and focus in your body, or have they also gotten less, or disappeared altogether? If you still have awareness of an intensity move your focus to something else, like a bird singing outside. Does the intensity change, get less or more? Interesting isn't it. This is how I know if the pain in a body is real or awareness of others...

Now gently bring your focus back to the room and your physical self, take a long gentle breath in and relaxing breath out...Has anything changed?

What do you notice, perceive, or receive from your body or surroundings?

Part of finding you, finding your potency and inner strength is acknowledging you are more than this body you have created.

Yes, you created your body, and continue to create it and uncreate it simply by the choices and conclusions you make every day. Your body is a reflection of your life, how you felt during it, your perceptions and judgements and conclusions you have made about yourself and what is possible (and what is not).

How many of you have been told..."You are too much!" or that "you need to tone it down!" or "Don't let people see you!" and so to fit in and be "Normal" you have contracted, folded and munched yourself down to be as small as everyone else around you? Did this work for you? Or do you still feel like a square peg trying to fit in a round hole. So...

"Everywhere you have defined what's possible, and what's impossible. Defined what you can show the world and this reality can you now let go...? Good!!

Everywhere that you still judge you as wrong for what you know should be possible, if you were allowed to simply be you, can you now let go and choose to let you be you and show up in totality...? Great!!

Remember in the "The Alchemist" (by Paulo Coelho), the King of Salem is talking to the young sheep herder about something called a personal legend and the king says...
"At this point in their lives everything is clear and everything is possible. They are not afraid to dream,

and to yearn for everything they would like to see happen to them in their lives. But, as time passes, a mysterious force begins to convince them that it will be impossible for them to realise their Personal Legend. **(Paulo Coelho. The Alchemist, pg 24, 25th Anniversary edition. 2014)**"

So, what if we have simply bought into this reality, turned off the dreams as not possible! Turned off the potency, and knowing, as not socially comfortable for others!! And made ourselves wrong to make everyone else feel right and justified...!!

Everywhere that you have chosen to make others more important and significant than yourself, can you now let go of that and choose to be the most important person in your life...? Thank you!

Everywhere that you make you, and your awareness, less significant than other people's thoughts, feelings, and emotions can you now please change that...? Let that choice go now, and choose to be you...regardless? Thank you.

What if being the potent being you really are is not dangerous to the world?

What if that is an implanted idea, and is just not true. I have had 3 people at different times sobbing on my table during their session as they tell me how they were single handedly responsible to the destruction of Lemuria, or Atlantis. That they have psychic memories of touching the crystal and seeing it explode and ultimately destroying the land they loved. And it is these memories that made them not want to be powerful in this lifetime. Interesting as two claimed to be the sole reason for the destruction…that no one else involved for the same place.

What if you being powerful and potent is only dangerous because you can't be controlled and kept small? Everywhere you have bought that you should be happy with what you have, and you are not supposed to ask for more…. Let that go!

Choose to be greater today than you were yesterday, so that your tomorrows can be even more…excellent.

Coming back to your judgements of you. Do you realise that your judgements of you, create your "Body". Quantum physics teaches us that our body reflects our past. Our past thoughts, feelings, and judgements about ourselves, and that when we change how we see, or think of ourselves, we change our body as we literally let go our past, which in turn changes how we show up in the future. So…

I invite you now to let go all your judgements and conclusions of what you are, what you are capable of creating and being, and even who you have defined yourself as with these judgements, and to begin creating from a new page, a new script, and begin a new story of you, of who, and what you can and will be.

What's all this got to do with you and me and potency of being? As much, or as little, as you choose. Let's stay on the positive line of thought. You have been practicing connection with the Earth, with the Universe, with each other, and even with the elements of creation, and still what is there? You have been exploring being the energy and space of Alchemy, or transformation (an invitation to change, a space without judgement). You have begun to get the sense of that infinite being we all hear we are. For some this space will be too much, fear will kick in, and you may choose to stop. Unfortunately, you have already begun to change who you are, so to return to where you were before is not really possible, as you really can't forget what you already know is possible. Now you are asking… "What do we do with this?"

The short answer is nothing! Just be you! Be the invitation for others to explore what is possible. Oh, and remember to be willing to be all energies! What's this "all energies" esoteric mumbo jumbo? Well how many of you have been taught that not only are you "too much" but the potency and strength of the potent kind are "bad", and that being meek, humble, and orderly are "good"?

What I see is that the Universe sees no difference between energies. Not good, not bad, not light nor dark… as these are judgements, and definitions, we have placed on them. A volcano erupting is great!

It creates new soil, and it releases pressure within the crust of the Earth, and even creates spectacular sunsets. We judge it as bad as we see trees get destroyed, animals die, and flights, and travel, and even our lives get disrupted. Crops don't grow so well for a year or two.

A night we call too dark is just perfect for a mouse trying to avoid the owl...

Are you now willing to be all the energies that are available to you? This doesn't mean you have to be them all the time. It simply means you no longer have to judge them as wrong and resist them, but now you can be them as required in the moment.

Everywhere you are unwilling to be the potent infinite Being embodied, because that has been judged as wrong, will you now choose to create with this potential and be that infinite Being embodied? Thank you.

Are you also willing to create from the space and energy of awareness and let go the old processes where you functioned on auto pilot, unconsciously and unaware? Thank you.

Yes, it's not easy. You will discover blocks *(Thoughts, conclusions, decisions, and even projections and expectations from others)* you didn't even know existed, and you may go through discomfort, doubt, and anger and blah blah blah as you work to let go and create change. Is it worth it? Only you can

That Book!

decide. Only you can choose for you. Only you can create the changes for you to begin to be all of you while finding your potency and potential...sorry.

On the bright side, look at all the fun you can have creating what you desire, being who, and what, brings you Joy. Even having the pleasure of seeing others benefit from your choices, as you invite them to create their own journey to transformation and change, as they discover their own buried potency within.

There are many, many, teachers, philosophers, and books out there to start you on your journey to meet you, but they can only start you. In the end you are the one who has to choose how far down the rabbit hole you want to go in this journey of self.

Oh, and while we are on the subject of self. This in itself is a contradiction and will keep you not liking yourself and constantly believing you are failing. Why do you say that Greg? Well for me this is a major cause of people feeling depressed as they realise they are not in touch with "Who and What" they are told is them...hahaha. What an insane thought... No, I mean it ...really.

We are raised by parents who are presenting a way of being to us as the correct and only way...grandparents who also have expectations and projections about who and what we are!! Then society also impels its rules and expectations on us. We also have all the conclusions we came to as we observed those

Gregory D Bryers MSc.

around us, listened to conversations *(that probably we heard out of context and still came to conclusions)*. All of this shapes the Us we think is us as we grow up and take shape. But...

WHAT ELSE IS THERE?

Underlying all of this is a knowing (well at least for me) that something else is possible. That all this is not me but there must be more... more is possible. Then we have teachers tell us that we create our reality. As we make choices, we open ourselves up to more possibilities. Neville Goddard, Napoleon Hill, and even recent authors and writers such as Louise Hay, Wayne Dyer all try to show us that our thoughts create our reality...so again... what is your "Authentic Self"?

There is a trilogy of books written under the Name of Jed McKenna called the Enlightenment Trilogy. That challenges you to look at all this. It challenges you to go into the attic of your mind and clear out the clutter of who you think you are. To discover who you are not...and let go. In book two he talks about the Hero's journey. He talks of and describes the story of Moby Dick and the amazing Captain Ahab. He puts it in another context...takes it away from just a story of a vengeful man to a man battling his demons within on his path to awakening, shaking off the shackles of old beliefs.

He talks of Luke Skywalker on his personal journey to wakeful awareness, another Hero's journey. He talks of an encounter with a group studying the Bhagdad-Gita and how they were studying it, but not seeing it, or understanding its real message as they separated themselves off, making themselves less than the hero. He shows a different way of reading these texts, or seeing the message within…what if we viewed these hero's as "our self"? We are the hero struggling to get past the limitations of our mind, training, entrainment. We are Arjuna! We are Luke! We are the reader and the subject. this is our battle!

On a personal note. A few years ago, I was a new student at university and had read all my required and optional text books (yeah, I know…nerdy but I was hungry for more knowing) and a lecturer was chatting with me about how I studied. She suggested I should read something totally unrelated to science, to help me find a balance so to speak. The next day, she brought book one of a series written by the Author David Eddings. The Belgariad series book one. I was hooked. Immediately I saw the journey to self…and I was captured by a single statement and the explanation given.

Learning to perform Magic the boy was struggling and his grandfather explained about the will and the word...explaining that if you desire something to happen you have to speak it and we tie this to an action...BOOM!!! My universe shouts at me...listen to this...If I desire something to happen...I must really desire it, must speak it, and then begin to create or do it...nothing doubting....

If you desire to change something in your body or life... again you have to think it, desire it and be it.... Neville Goddard puts it this way...wishes already fulfilled!! See it from your eyes as already there... not from the point of view of the spectator...The Bible tells us... "As a man thinketh so is he!" So, when we ask for something and then think... "oh well maybe another time..." That's exactly what we create...another time!!

I'm still working on this issue within myself as I let go my past and making my present less significant and important... (haha doesn't that sound special....?). What if time was irrelevant and not real? Quantum physics peeps like Gregg Braden teach us that we can change our past and our future by the choices we make now. Here is a little taste of what I mean...

So, get comfortable! Now think about something that you are grateful for. Something that makes you smile every time you think of it... something that makes your heart beat faster from the shear joy and pleasure remembered!

Now, in your mind take yourself there! To that moment in time and see yourself as though from the view point of an onlooker, a spectator. Keep feeling that joy!! and flow the joy you feel to the "You" that you are watching...does this change anything for you? Its ok if it doesn't...this crap is not for everyone (I just found it works for me). My point of view and my emotional memories of a very difficult time have changed in ways that have surprised me. I have more ease with it all. The anger that was hidden inside is much less and I have more ease with me.

Recently I started visiting the little me outside of the village I grew up in. The morning after our mother was beaten unconscious in front of us, and was now missing, and no one (the adults) were talking. I used to visit him and feel his confusion, his anger, and even his inability to help his mother. Then I saw how this was making me more of this anger....so... I decided to visit him with a different purpose and a different energy.

I take myself there, standing beside him, and I feel all the joy and gratitude I can for him, his strength to keep on existing. I thank him for the life I have now and I radiate this gratitude to him and I let him know he makes it. I let him know his mother lives, that his father gets what he creates for himself.

This has had a profound effect on me, as I also let go the little boy lost and unwanted. The little boy who is different and the wrongness that all his past created.

The people who follow Neville Goddard's work say that we can change the past and present by doing a "Re-vision" of an event. Take yourself back to the event and visualise a different outcome and feel the energy and emotions of the different outcome! You see it's the emotions we attach to the story that hold us there...and as our past is no longer real... it's in the past ... We can look at it and create a different story and change how we "feel" about it. *A strange thing happens as you really let go the past. Your body changes and even you face changes.*

I guess what I have been attempting to tell and show you is, there is choice. Sometimes, it is only a choice of how we deal with something, other times it is a choice of what we would enjoy creating, or how we look back at what we created. So much of this is my reality and doesn't mean you must embrace it to become healthy, or creative. You don't have to do anything. Its more than ok.

Gregory D Bryers MSc.

A last "Word"

A few authors whom I respect and enjoy have said… "When someone tells you that you must do this! and then this will happen…run! Get out of there!" and I agree with them. So, you have read this and now you get to choose what works (if anything works) for you and what you can throw away. This started out as a way to show how I got "Better" and recovered my wellbeing… haha and has been more a self-healing for petit moi. A rather cathartic adventure I must admit.

Thank you for reading it and I hope it gives you hope or a direction to begin your own journey to self. And remember… the "Self" of today will be different to the "Self" of tomorrow based on choices you make today…or not!

Greg

IMPRINT

© Gregory Bryers

1st edition 2019

All rights reserved.
Reproduction, in whole or in part, is prohibited.
No part of this work may be reproduced, reproduced or distributed in any form without written permission from the author.
Contact: Gregory Bryers / Herrenstr. 22/3062 Kirchstetten

Cover design: kindle cover creator

Printed in Great Britain
by Amazon